JAMES WISEMAN

STOBI.

A GUIDE TO THE EXCAVATIONS.

BEOGRAD 1973

Published by the University of Texas at Austin and the National Museum of Titov Veles with a publication grant from the Smithsonian Institution.

FOR THE PUBLISCHER

TIHO NAJDOVSKI

EDITORIAL ASSISTANT

ANA PREMK

For

DJORDJE MANO-ZISSI

TABLE OF CONTENTS

6

Cover emblem design by *Žika Radošević*

NOTES A

Most of the build
oriented southeast-northv
the buildings are consid
directions are adjusted t
tation of monuments an
north arrows on the pla

The numbers in
the *Guide* are keyed to
back of the book.

Dates before Chr
B. C., "before Christ".
"anno Domini" ("in the
or A. C., "after Christ"

A few other stan
liographies.

AA

AJA

BIABulg

PREFACE

The *Guide* was written during the late summer
of 1972. During its composition I had the opportu-
nity to consult members of the Excavation Staff on
several matters regarding the history and monuments
of Stobi. I am grateful to the entire staff, an extraor-
dinarily talented and diligent group of scholars, and
especially to Djordje Mano-Zissi, Co-Director with me
at Stobi, for his sage advice and constant encourage-
ment. Kenneth Sams and Al B. Wesolowsky read an
earlier draft of the *Guide* and the work was improved
by their thoughtful comments. Special gratitude
should also be acknowledged for help in various ways
to Lucy Wiseman, Ellen C. Schwartz and Žika Radošević. Ana Premk was our conscientious editorial
assistant who saw the work through the press.

The Stobi Museum was planned by the Co-
-Directors along with Ranko Findrih, Todor Gruev,
Ivan Mikulčić, Tiho Najdovski, Lucy Wiseman and
Ruth Ziser. David B. Peck was especially helpful in
drawings and designs for the interior remodelling and

construction o
burial display
Staff also pro

The *Gu*
Texas at Aus
Veles, the spc
vation Project
and with the
Institution.

Austin, Texas
October 14, 1

DenkschrWien Phil-hist Kl.	K. Akademie der Wissenschaften, Wien. Philosophische-historische Klasse. Denkschriften.
DOPapers	Dumbarton Oaks Papers.
JÖAI	Jahreshefte des österreichischen archäologischen Instituts.
RA	Revue Archéologique.
WJh	Wiener Jahreshefte.
ZNTW	Zeitschrift für die neutestamentliche Wissenschaft und die Kunde des alteren Kirche.

LIST OF ILLUSTRATIONS

8. Dancing Satyr from the Theodosian Palace. Photo courtesy of the National Museum of Belgrade.

9. Drinking Satyr from the Theodosian Palace. Photo courtesy of the National Museum of Belgrade.

10. Sketch Plan of the House of the Fuller. Drawing by David B. Peck after Milorad Čorluka and Petar Nikušef.

11. House of the Fuller. View of the hypocaust from the south. Photo by Tom Eals.

12. Episcopal Basilica. The later mosaic in the south aisle. Watercolor by M. Petrovski and B. Damjanovski.

13. Baptistery. Drawing of the mosaic by William B. Dinsmoor, Jr.

14. Baptistery. Portrait face in fresco. Photo by Tom Eals.

15. Terracotta figurine of Telesphorus from Grave 21 of the West Cemetery. Photo by Richard Trimble.

16. Theater. Plan by William B. Dinsmoor, Jr.

17. Theater. View of cavea from the north parodos. Photo by Tom Eals.

18. Statue of a Roman Emperor. Photo by James Wiseman.

19. Plan of the Casino. Traced by B. O. Davis from a photograph of a drawing by the staff architect of 1940.

20. Plan of the Cemetery Basilica. Traced by B. O. Davis from a photograph of a plan by Ivan N. Petrović with an addition by David B. Peck.

21. Plan of the Palikura Basilica. From R. F. Hoddinott, *Early Byzantine Churches in Macedonia and Southern Serbia* (London and New York, 1963), Fig. 95. Tracing and addition of narthex by David B. Peck.

At end of Guide:

Plan of Site. Surveyed and drawn by Paul Huffman (1971) and David B. Peck (1972).

HISTORICAL SKETCH

The earliest preserved literary reference to Stobi records a victory of Philip V, King of Macedonia, over the Dardanians "in the vicinity of Stobi of Paeonia" in 197 B. C. (Livy XXXIII. 19. 3). The historian Livy, in another passage, locates Stobi on the Erigon (Crna) River not far from where that river empties into the Axius (Vardar) and calls it an "old city", contrasting it with the new city of Perseis which Philip V founded in 183 B. C. (Livy XXXIX. 53. 14—16).

The archaeological evidence for the founding of the city is still somewhat meager but does support a Hellenistic date not far removed from the time of Philip V. Stratified deposits of the late 3rd and 2nd centuries B. C. have been revealed by tests on the acropolis and below several buildings near the center of the later city. A few objects, chiefly small bronzes, that date to the Classical and Archaic periods have occasionally been found at Stobi but have not been associated with equally early contextual material. In the light of the present evidence, it seems likely that Stobi was founded during the century following the operations of Philip II against the Paeonians in 359 B. C. (Diodorus XVI. 4).

Macedonia was divided into four regions after the Roman victory over the Macedonian King Perseus in 168 B. C. and Stobi was made the salt emporium of the third region (Livy XLV. 29. 13). Macedonia became a Roman province in 148 B. C. but there is no evidence yet for any drastic change of life at Stobi at that time. It was not until the reign of Augustus (31 B. C. — A. D. 14) that the city shows a marked change in extent, doubtlessly reflecting a significant increase in population. The Hellenistic cemetery in the area of the House of Peristerias was covered over and structures erected there, as well as further to the south and west, perhaps as far as the later city wall. Some 55 graves, at any rate, which date to the time of Augustus were excavated in 1970—71, not far to the southwest of the Porta Heraclea, and were found to lie on virgin soil. This area just outside the city gate, designated the West Cemetery by the excavators, continued to function as an important burial ground until the late 4th century after Christ. No graves of Early Imperial date have yet been found within the limits of the city walls.

This radical expansion of the city may be associated with a rise in status to the rank of *municipium*, a title it certainly possessed by A. D. 69 when Stobi began to mint its own coins in a variety of types with

the legend *municipium Stobensium*. Stobi continued to issue coins at least until the early 3rd century. There are also occasional references in ancient literature and in a number of inscriptions that confirm the status of Stobi as a *municipium*. What is more, its citizens also enjoyed the *ius Italicum;* that is, they were citizens of Rome (Pliny nat. hist. IV. 10. 34) and were registered in the Roman tribes Aemilia and Tromentina.

During the Early and Middle Imperial periods the city was evidently a prosperous and flourishing community. Numerous inscribed monuments attest the public or religious beneficence of some of its wealthier citizens. A large building near the East City Wall, with elaborately molded stucco and figured fresco on its interior walls, provides some idea of this early prosperity. The Sanctuary of Nemesis in the theater is the only sanctuary that has so far been discovered; we can, however, be sure of numerous other holy places within the city. Among the gods worshipped were Asclepius, Hygieia and Telesphorus; Artemis Lochia; Clarian Apollo; the cult of the Emperors; Jupiter Liberator; Dionysus; and Hera.

The most prominent monument of the Roman city now visible is the theater, which was built in the 2nd or early 3rd century A. C. The marble seats of the cavea are covered with the inscribed names of the patrons both of the theater and of the games held there when the structure was converted into an arena. The seats provide, therefore, an important basis for

the study of family names and relationships at Stobi, especially during the 3rd century.

Stobi was perhaps an even more properous and influential town during the Early Christian period. The city was the seat of a bishop at least by A. D. 325 when Budius, Bishop of Stobi, attended the Council of Nicaea. During the 4th and 5th centuries no fewer than three Christian basilicas were constructed within the limits of the city, two of which possessed baptisteries, while at least two more lay outside the city to the southwest and perhaps another to the east across the Erigon.

The City Wall was in existence at least by the 3rd century, and the Inner Wall along the east seems to have been constructed late in the 4th century when the outer wall on the east was abandoned. The lines of both walls are clear and may be traced almost throughout their extent along the ridges that mark their circuit. The Inner Wall was evidently constructed after repeated flooding along the left bank of the Erigon had made that area unsafe for habitation. The new wall would have afforded more protection against the damaging floods of the Erigon. The river, indeed, was brought under control only in 1969 when a dam was built some 20 kilometers upriver.

The churches of Stobi were splendid monuments with frescoes and mosaics, many of which have been found in a remarkably good state of preservation. It is likely that the city was the home of major fresco and mosaic schools. Fine mosaics were not limited

to the churches, but were laid also in some of the sumptuous private residences, such as the House of Peristerias and the Theodosian Palace.

A Jewish community of some wealth existed in Stobi at least by the 3rd century when Polycharmus, "the father of the Synagogue", built a synagogue nearly in the center of the city. The synagogue was rebuilt again on what was evidently an even more lavish scale early in the following century. A mosaic floor with geometric designs was added and the walls of the main room were covered with frescoes. The synagogue was destroyed in the late 4th century and a Christian basilica erected upon its ruins.

The conversion of a place holy to the Jewish community into the site of a Christian church took place about the time of the visit of the Emperor Theodosius I to Stobi. He issued two edicts from Stobi during June, A. D. 388, forbidding the assembly of heretics and any public discussion of religion (Codex Theodosianus 16. 4. 2, 5. 15).

Other bishops of Stobi are known from the 5th century: Nicolaus, who attended the Council of Chalcedon in 451, and Philip, whose name was recorded on the lintel of the nave of the Episcopal Basilica. Perhaps the most famous inhabitant of Stobi, Ioannes Stobaeus, whose scholarly studies have been preserved to modern times, had his home and library at Stobi during the same century.

Stobi may have become the capital of Macedonia Salutaris when that province was organized in the

late 4th century. Certainly she was the capital of Second Macedonia following the 5th century reorganization of provincial boundaries (Hierocles 10). Stobi was called an ἄποικος (colony) of the Romans by Stephanus of Byzantium, but there is no other evidence for that title and the accuracy of Stephanus here has recently been questioned.

The later 5th century was a time of disaster for Stobi. In 472 the city escaped ruin by opening its gates to Theodemir, King of the Ostrogoths, but must have paid heavily in money and supplies for the Ostrogothic army that was then marching on Constantinople. In 479 the city was less fortunate and was sacked by the army of Theoderic, son and heir of Theodemir (Malchus 18). The city only partially recovered during the next generation before it was struck by a new disaster, the great earthquake of 518 (Marcellinus Comes 100).

The city never again recovered its former prosperity. Phocas, Bishop of Stobi, attended the Council of Constantinople in 553, but in less than two decades after that event the citizens abandoned their city, perhaps in fear of the spreading plague that afflicted the eastern empire in mid-century, or they may have fled at the time of the Slavic invasions in the late 6th century. In any case, the city appears to have been at least partially deserted at the time of its final destruction. Before the collapse of the great buildings, the handsome mosaic of the Baptistery on the south side of the Episcopal Basilica was dug through merely

to remove the lead pipe that once had brought water to the piscina; and the adjacent crypt was plundered of all it contained.

The latest coins in the final destruction levels both in the houses on the acropolis and in the ecclesiastical structures south of the Episcopal Basilica date to the 5th year of the reign of Justin II (A. D. 569——570). It is not yet possible to say with certainty whether that destruction was natural or brought about by an invading army. In view of the known movements of Slavic forces and other northern peoples at that time, the latter is indeed likely.

Two other bishops of Stobi are known from the 7th century and there is a reference to the destruction of a military garrison at Stobi by Basil II in A. D. 1014 (Cedrenus, p. 709). But neither circumstance reguires the presence of an urban community; there are numerous examples of bishops holding sees they never visited and a military outpost is hardly evidence for a town. The archaeological remains do indicate some activity in the upper levels of the theater during the 11th century and several Slavic graves have been excavated in the vicinity of the North Basilica. But there is no trace of settled habitation at Stobi after the 6th century.

BIBLIOGRAPHY. Balduin Saria, "Stobi", *Narodna Enciklopedija Srpsko-Hrvatsko Slovenačka* 4 (1929) 489—491; *idem*, "Stobi", *Real-Encyclopedie* 4A (1932) 47—54. Ernst Kitzinger, "The Early Christian Town of Stobi," *DOPapers* 3 (1946) 81——161. James Wiseman and Djordje Mano-Zissi, "Excavations at Stobi, 1970," *AJA* 75 (1971) 395—411 and "Excavations at Stobi, 1971", *AJA* 76 (1972) 407—424. Dj. Mano-Zissi, "Stobi," *Enciklopedija Jugoslavije* 8, Leksikografski zavod Zagreb (1971) 153—155.

THE EXCAVATIONS

The location of the ancient city on the left bank of the Crna River where it flows into the Vardar was first recognized in the 1850s and 1860s by J. G. von Hahn and Leon Heuzey who were involved in independent travel and research. Excavation, however, did not follow immediately. There were brief investigations at the site in 1902 by A. von Premerstein and N. Vulić which resulted chiefly in the recording of a number of inscriptions. During the First World War German soldiers exposed parts of the Episcopal Basilica, the Cemetery Basilica and the Palikura Basilica, but it was only in 1924 that systematic excavation was undertaken. In that year the National Museum of Belgrade began a series of excavations that continued annually until 1934. Work at the site continued on a smaller scale after that date until 1940 under the sponsorship of the Prince Paul Museum (the name of the National Museum at Belgrade for a brief period).

These early excavations resulted in the uncovering of a large section of the western and central parts of the ancient city, but were concerned chiefly with structures of the latest phase of occupation. The most important areas excavated or partially cleared during those years were the Episcopal Basilica, the theater, the Via Sacra and part of the Porta Heraclea, the Episcopal Residence, the Synagogue Basilica and the adjacent residence, the baths, and three large private dwellings now called the Theodosian Palace, the House of Parthenius, and the House of Peristerias. Numerous other buildings were also explored.

Since 1955 there have been occasional, short--term excavations at Stobi. These more recent investigations were usually either concerned with problems of individual monuments or carried out in conjunction with conservation work at the site. The latter projects, sponsored by the Conservation Institute of Macedonia, included the partial restoration of the Synagogue Basilica and the adjacent residence (House of Psalms), the large and small baths and the central fountain as well as the discovery of the mosaic of the synagogue below the Synagogue Basilica. The Conservation Institute also uncovered additional sections of the theater. The other excavations were performed chiefly by the Archaeological Museum of Skopje and the principal buildings investigated were the North Basilica, the Civil Basilica, lower levels in the House of Peristerias, and a private residential area west of the Synagogue Basilica.

The University of Texas at Austin and the National Museum of Titov Veles, under the sponsorship of the Smithsonian Institution, began a new series of annual excavations in 1970. The new Stobi Excavation Project has undertaken to complete the excavation and study of several buildings begun by earlier excavators, such as the theater, the Episcopal Basilica and the Synagogue Basilica, and at the same time to test the ful extent of the city both in time and space. These investigations have greatly increased our knowledge about the founding of the city, its growth over nearly 900 years, the location and form of the city walls, and they have brought about the discovery of several monuments and buildings belonging to all periods of the life of the ancient city. Among the latter are the Baptistery south of the Episcopal Basilica, the Synagogue of Polycharmus (3rd century after Christ), and the large buildings of the Early Imperial city discovered in 1972 near the left bank of the Crna River.

BIBLIOGRAPHY. The results of the excavations performed through 1971 are discussed in the sources cited in the bibliographies at the end of each section of the *Guide*. See also J. G. von Hahn, "Reise von Belgrad nach Salonik," *Denkschr Wien Phil-hist Kl.* 11, pt. 2 (1861) 175, 231—236; *idem*," Reise durch die Gebiete des Drin und Wardar", *ibid.*, 15, pt. 2 (1867) 158—188. Leon Heuzey, "Découverte des Ruines de Stobi", *RA* 2 (1873) 25—42. See also Dj. Mano-Zissi, "Stratigraphic Problems and the Urban Development of Stobi", in the forthcoming *Studies in the Antiquities of Stobi*, Vol. 1, Beograd 1973. B. Josifovska, *Vodič niz Stobi*, Skopje 1953.

A VISIT TO THE SITE

A visit to the Stobi Museum (27), which is located to the right of the entrance gate, affords a good introduction to the history and topography of the city, and is the recommended beginning for a tour of Stobi.

An earthen road leads south from the Museum and continues directly across the site. The visitor setting out from the Museum should take the first path that ascends to the right of the earthen road to arrive at the Via Principalis Inferior (9) which provides access to the North Basilica (1), Civil Basilica (2), Synagogue Basilica (4), and House of Psalms (5). Beyond the House of Psalms the line of the ancient street crosses the Via Axia (6) and passes between the Central Fountain (7) and the Large Bath (8). The street ascends slightly as it approaches the Via Theodosia (11) where the visitor might turn to the right, after visiting the Theodosian Palace (12), and continue to the Via Principalis Superior (14).

Along the upper street lie the House of the Fuller (15) and the entrance to the Episcopal Residence

(16). Beyond an angled turn lies the colonnaded Via Sacra (18) that leads to the Porta Heraclea (21). From here there is a good view to the south and southwest where the West Cemetery (22), the Cemetery Basilica (28) and the Palikura Basilica (29) are located.

The main entrance to the Episcopal Basilica (19) is on the east side of the Via Sacra. After visiting the Baptistery (20) on the terrace below the basilica to the south, the visitor should return to the upper level at the southeastern corner of the basilica for a view of the theater (23). There is a path that descends to the right behind the theater which leads to the scene building and the orchestra.

From the theater the road to the Museum passes the Casino (24) on the left. A path to the right, opposite the Synagogue Basilica, leads to the recently excavated sections of the City Walls and the Turkish Bridge (26).

THE MONUMENTS

1. NORTH BASILICA. Fig. 1.

The basilica was entered in antiquity by descending one of the two flights of stairs leading from the Via Principalis Inferior into the exonarthex at the western end of the church. The atrium is a tripartite space between the two stairways; it is separated from the exonarthex by two marble columns and the heavy piers of the stairs. The atrium consists of two exedras on either side of a basin, above which are three marble encrusted niches. The central niche is pierced by a water spout. The exonarthex, which is paved with sandstone slabs, has doorways on the north and south leading to side chambers and, on the east, columns frame each of the two doorways that lead to the narthex.

The floor of the narthex in its last period consists simply of baked bricks. The drain of the atrium, covered with stone slabs, can be seen crossing the north side of the narthex and extending the length of the north aisle. A narrow doorway connects the narthex with each of the two side aisles and a wide central opening with two columns provides access to the nave.

The main body of the basilica has a broad nave separated from the two side aisles by colonnades of unfluted marble columns with Corinthian capitals. The stylobates for the colonnades were made chiefly from marble theater seats and the worn remnants of a few inscriptions can still be seen on them. Only one complete name, Ἡρακλ(ε)ίδης, is preserved (the seat block re-used beneath the fourth column from the west in the south aisle). The colonnades frame a semicircular apse.

There are two chambers each on the north and south sides of the basilica, and can be reached both from the narthex and exonarthex. The chambers on the north were, in addition, themselves connected by a doorway. The northern room entered from the narthex was provided with a bench, and part of a mosaic existed at the time of the original excavation in 1937. The mosaic depicted Christian symbols in square panels separated by a cable pattern. This room has a third doorway which leads into the baptistery for which it must have served as an anteroom.

The small baptistery is quatrefoil in shape and paved with bricks and marble slabs. A cruciform piscina, which is centered in the room, was encrusted with marble and on its parapet stood four red porphyry columns to carry a ciborium. A doorway through the southern apse gives directly onto the north aisle of the basilica.

The date of the basilica is uncertain because of a lack of contextual material from the early excavations. The late 5th to early 6th centuries has been suggested on the basis of architectural style. An additional problem in dating arises from the fact that a baptistery was an adjunct only of an episcopal basilica in the early years of the church, and the Basilica of the Bishop Philip (19), with its adjacent baptistery, was also in use during the 5th and 6th centuries.

The area became a cemetery in the mediaeval period. A total of 23 graves dated to the 9th to 12th centuries were found in 1955 just south of the basilica near its eastern end.

BIBLIOGRAPHY. Jozo Petrović, "U Stobima danas", *Glasnik Hrvatskih zemaljskih muzeja u Sarajevu, 1942* (Sarajevo 1943) 28—34. D. Koco *et al.*, "Izveštaj za iskopavanjata vo Stobi", *Zbornik na Arheološkiot Muzej, Skopje* (1961) 69—72. R. F. Hoddinott, *Early Byzantine Churches in Macedonia and Southern Serbia* (London and New York 1963) 168—169.

2. CIVIL BASILICA.

Between the North Basilica and the Synagogue Basilica are the poorly preserved remains of another basilica. No evidence for its use as a church was found by the original excavators in 1937 nor by the archaeologists who investigated the site further in 1956—57.

The excavators, who identified seven building phases, suggested that it may ultimately have served some civic function and so named the structure the Civil Basilica.

Some of the earliest material yet found in Stobi was unearthed below the level of the Civil Basilica. A few small bronzes dating to the early 5th century B.C. were found in a deep test trench within the apse dug during the 1930s. A fresco depicting water birds and dating perhaps to the early 1st century A. C. was removed from a wall deep below the nave of the basilica during the 1950s. Hellenistic deposits were also found at that time and excavations in 1971 and 1972 revealed other Hellenistic habitation levels (3rd to 2nd centuries B. C.). The Hellenistic deposits lie immediately above the prehistoric bed of the Crna River.

BIBLIOGRAPHY. Jozo Petrović, "U Stobima danas", *Glasnik hrvatskih zemaljskih muzeja u Sarajevu, 1942* (Sarajevo 1943) 486. James Wiseman and Djordje Mano-Zissi, "Excavations at Stobi, 1971", *AJA* 76 (1972) Section 4.

3. LITTLE BATH.

The principal entrance to the Little Bath is at its northwest corner where a flight of four steps leads down from the narrow lane that separates the Synagogue Basilica from the Civil Basilica. The room entered here, the apodyterium, is a large rectangular space with a square base, perhaps for a pier, in the center of the room. To the right of the entrance three steps lead down into an apsidal plunge.

South of the plunge is the double-room of the hypocaust with three apses on the south side. The westernmost apse of the three contained a water basin and there may have been similar arrangements in the other two. The hypocaust piers were made both of circular and square bricks. The brick and concrete vaulted tunnel by which the hot air was brought into the hypocaust area pierces the central southern apse and four similar passages allowed the circulation of heat beneath the floor to the east.

There is a rectangular room west of the hypocaust whose function is unknown and another stone-paved room to the east which served as a secondary entranceway with a door opening to the exterior on the south. The latrine is in the northeast corner and could be reached directly from the outside by a small doorway on the south side.

4. SYNAGOGUE BASILICA. Fig. 2.

The Christian basilica that lies immediately south of the Civil Basilica was also entered from the Via Principalis Inferior. The threshold of the single doorway is still in place and a short stairway leads to a corridor that surrounds a colonnaded courtyard. There

is a water basin along the west side of the courtyard
and the court itself, which was paved with flagstones
only over the southwestern part, was entered from
the northern hall. This area, the atrium of the basilica, is not centered on the axis of the basilica because
a part of the width is occupied by two rooms on the
west.

Two doorways lead from the atrium to the narthex where part of the original flagstone paving is
preserved. A wide doorway and two narrower doors
lead into the nave and two side aisles of the basilica.
The floor of the nave in its final period was paved
with sandstone slabs; a part of the base for the chancel screen is still preserved in place. There were five
columns in each of the colonnades that separated nave
from side aisle and a total of 8 bases can still be seen
in their original positions. The bases are of different
styles and sizes and are vivid reminders that later
architecture at Stobi was highly eclectic; many buildings, including this basilica, utilized architectural
pieces from a variety of earlier buildings.

The basilica was constructed in the late 4th or
early 5th century and was remodelled at least once
late in that century, probably following he Gothic
destruction of A. D. 479. The immediate predecessor
of the Christian church was a synagogue whose mosaic floor was discovered over 1.5 meters below the
floor of the nave. Most of the mosaic below the nave
has been removed and set in concrete blocks prepara-
tory to its eventual reconstitution. Other sections of

the mosaic are still in place below the north aisle, be ow the narthex and at the entranceway into the courtyard of the atrium. The brick and concrete foundation visible at the eastern end of the synagogue below the nave probably supported the chest in which the Torah was contained. Parts of the synagogue walls, wh ch were covered with fresco and molded stucco, are visible below the north aisle and below the nave near the south stylobate. A room at the southwest, which was later cut through by the nave-narthex wall of the basilica, provided access to the contiguous building to the south (5).

The synagogue just described had been built in the early 4th century and utilized some of the walls of a 3rd century synagogue which we may now associate definitely with Tiberius Claudius Polycharmus, "the father of the synagogue at Stobi." The name Polycharmus has been known since the discovery in 1931 of a column bearing a lengthy inscription detailing the work performed at his expense during the construction of the synagogue. The column had been re-used in the northeast corner of the colonnade in the atrium of the basilica and thereby led some scholars to suppose that the Christian basilica was a synagogue. Recent excavations below the mosaic floor of the later synagogue resulted in the discovery of only a few architectural elements of the 3rd century structure (a threshold, a few floor paving slabs), but did reveal numerous pieces of a fresco with the repeated Greek legend Πολύχαρμος ὁ πατὴρ εὐχήν ("Polycharmus, the father, as a votive offering"). Pottery and coins found with the fresco date to the 3rd century after Christ.

A still earlier synagogue may be represented by a flagstone paving found in deeper tests below the nave in 1970 and 1971 and by an impressively heavy, stone-paved floor discovered in a small test trench below the north hall of the atrium in 1972. The pottery found on both floors dated to the 1st century of our era.

Deeper tests in 1971 below the narthex brought to light part of a structure of the 2nd century B. C. and, later in the same season, a hoard of silver coins was found below the nave. The coins ranged in date from 211 to 125 B. C. (Fig. 3) and included 506 Roman denarii, one victoriatus and a single Attic tetradrachma. They had been placed in two vessels, a coarse jug and a small lekythos, and hidden in a pit at a level not far below the synagogue of Polycharmus. These deposits of the Hellenistic period lay directly upon the prehistoric river bed.

BIBLIOGRAPHY. Jozo Petrović, "Iskopavanje u Stobima 1931", *Starinar* 7 (1932) 81—86, 135—136; *idem*, "Stobi, 1932", *Starinar* 8—9 (1933—1934) 169—191. Ernst Kitzinger, "A Survey of the Early Christian Town of Stobi," *DOPapers* 3 (1946) 129—146. Martin Hengel, "Die Synagogeninschrift von Stobi", *ZNTW* 57 (1966) 145—183. James Wiseman and Djordje Mano-Zissi, "Excavations at Stobi, 1970", *AJA* 75 (1971) 406—411 and "Excavations at Stobi, 1971", *AJA* 76 (1972) Section 3.

5. HOUSE OF PSALMS.

The large residence on the south side of the
Synagogue Basilica was reached directly from the
basilica through a doorway that leads from the west
hall of the atrium into a small room in the upper
storey of the residence. The ground floor was reached
by a narrow stairway descending to the east. The
chief entrance, however, was from a colonnaded portico on the Via Axia (6) where a doorway opens
onto a small foyer. This room and the other rooms
at the western end of the building were paved with
flagstones and were intended as service and access
areas.

Beyond the entrance foyer a broad stairway descends to a corridor on the right which passes between
a rectangular room and the south side of a colonnaded
courtyard. Both the corridor and the room are paved
with mosaics which bear simple geometric designs.
The hall east of the courtyard has a similar mosaic
pavement. A large water basin with columns and niches
forms the western side of the courtyard and there is
a well near the southeastern corner.

The large apsidal room which is entered from the
eastern colonnade is paved with a mosaic of more
intricate design (Fig. 4) than those of the hallways.
The mosaic is divided into four main areas. The
westernmost contains geometric designs, birds, chal-
ices and other objects in small, tightly restricted panels. To the east larger registers with water birds

among foliage frame an octagonal fountain which was built into the center of the room. The largest panel lies immediately east and depicts deer and water birds at a kantharos which overflows with water. The design and technique are identical with the mosaic in the Baptistery of the Episcopal Basilica and must have been made by the same artist. There are geometric designs again, chiefly a scales pattern, in the apse itself.

There are storerooms adjacent to the apsidal room on the north, and on the south a hallway provides access to a large stone-paved room that may have served as private quarters. A steep flight of four steps leads from the large room to a latrine built on the level of the Via Axia. The floor and drain slope to the east and would connect with the drain coming from the Large Bath (8) before continuing on to join the drain of the Little Bath (3).

The religious nature of the mosaic in the apsidal room and the fact that the building is tied structurally to the basilica suggest that the residence belonged to the church itself, perhaps serving as a rectory. But the building also communicated directly with at least one of the synagogues that preceded the basilica; a large sandstone threshold is still in place in the north peristyle and was built over by the south wall of the basilica. The House of Psalms clearly served successively the Jewish and Christian communities of Stobi.

A marble monument bearing a Latin inscription in honor of A. Pontius Quietus now stands in the north colonnade near where it was discovered in the excavations of 1932. The statue of a Roman matron, which was found the same year in the fountain of the courtyard, is in the National Museum of Belgrade.

BIBLIOGRAPHY. Jozo Petrović, "Stobi 1932", *Starinar* 8—9 (1933—1934) 169—191. Ernst Kitzinger, "A Survey of the Early Christian Town of Stobi", *DOPapers* 3 (1946) 134—140. James Wiseman and Djordje Mano-Zissi, "Excavations at Stobi, 1970", *AJA* 75 (1971) 406—411.

6. VIA AXIA.

The Via Axia (about 4.5 meters wide) was one of the principal east-west streets of the city. Only the portion of it that lies between the House of Psalms (5) and the Large Bath (8) has so far been excavated, but it would have continued to the west alongside the northern facade of the House of Peristerias (10).

7. CENTRAL FOUNTAIN.

A small, stone-paved piazza opens to the south from the Via Axia at the intersection of the Via Principalis Inferior. On the west side of the piazza, backed against one of the walls of the House of Peristerias, is a fountain of simple design which was intended to serve the general public.

Water poured into three stone basins through spouts set into all three inner faces of the bracket-shaped reservoir. The basins rest on architectural pieces re-used from the theater and other earlier buildings. The fountain itself was supplied by water from the aqueduct that lies under the Via Principalis Inferior. The source of the water carried in the aqueduct was outside the city to the southwest, perhaps as far distant as the spring at the village of Rosoman, where antiquities have been found, although the near-by spring known today as Gradska Češma was probably also utilized.

The Central Fountain, both baths (3 and 8) and the House of Psalms (5) were partially restored by the Conservation Institute of Macedonia during the 1960s.

8. LARGE BATH.

The Large Bath was excavated in 1931 and 1932 and investigated further during the restoration of the structure in the 1960s. The principal entrance is from the Via Axia near the western end of the building. Here, as in the Little Bath, one enters a large room that served as the apodyterium. There is a bench along the marble encrusted walls except in the east and in the southeast where a broad stairway descends two steps to a nearly square room with two niches, probably for statuettes. A third niche was set into the east wall of the room at the top of the stairway just mentioned.

The large room of the hypocaust has a single, central apse on the east and is entered from the main room via a raised platform. The floor was paved with marble and remains of six marble water basins were located both in and to both sides of the apse. The furnace was on the south.

The main room also provided access at the same lower level to two rooms on the south, the second of which also had an entrance from the Via Axia. A large latrine is located in the northeast corner.

The complex of walls to the south and east of the Large Bath belong to structures only partially explored by the early excavators and the nature of the buildings to which they belong is still unclear. There is an earlier building, perhaps also a bath, immediately below the Large Bath and openings that provide a glimpse of that structure have been left by the conservators in the floor of the apodyterium and in the platform west of the room of the hypocaust.

The bath as restored was evidently in use during the final phase of the city in the late 6th century after Christ. The statue of a bearded man found in the apodyterium, however, seems to date to the Middle Imperial Period, and a statue of Venus found east of the triangular courtyard area south of the bath is perhaps even earlier. Both statues are now in the National Museum of Belgrade.

BIBLIOGRAPHY. Jozo Petrović, "Stobi 1932", *Starinar* 8—9 (1933—1934) 169—191. Ernst Kitzinger, "A Survey of the Early Christian Town of Stobi", *DOPapers* 3 (1946) 140—141.

9. VIA PRINCIPALIS INFERIOR.

The Early Christian city of Stobi, as well as the earlier Roman city, was built in a series of terraces descending from the top of the low ridge that marks the site to the flood plain of the present Crna River. The terraces are separated by the chief north-south streets of the city, the Via Principalis Inferior and Superior (14). The streets, therefore, lay at the approximate ground level of most buildings to the west and usually some height above the structures to the east. In the latter case stairways led down from the street, frequently into courtyards.

The Via Principalis Inferior can be followed from the northwest corner of the North Basilica (1) to the Central Fountain (7) beyond which it lies at a slightly higher level above an aqueduct. The street continues to the south passing the House of Peristerias (10), the Theodosian Palace (12) and the House of Parthenius (13). Immediately south of the House of Parthenius the aqueduct supplied water for a basin in a small paved court reached by descending a few steps to the west. The court may be another piazza, similar to the one by the Central Fountain, marking the intersection of another east-west street with the Via Principalis Inferior.

The street has not yet been traced further south, though the modern path that ascends to the area east of the Episcopal Basilica probably follows the line of the ancient way.

10. HOUSE OF PERISTERIAS.

The large complex referred to as the House of Peristerias may not be a single residential unit, but several, perhaps providing quarters for a number of related families. It is likely, too, that some of the rooms to the west were even completely separate and may have been occupied by small shops or have served as lodgings for less wealthy citlzens. It is in any case convenient for reference to designate as the House of Peristerias that architectural complex bounded on the east and west by the Via Principalis Superior (14) and Inferior (9), and on the north and south by the Via Axia (6) and the Via Theodosia (11).

The family of Peristerias certainly occupied at least the buildings in the southern half of the area, as we learn from an inscription in a mosaic floor, and it is this area that provides the more interesting architectural arrangements. An open courtyard with a large fountain along its western side provides a central, unifying element. The back wall of the basin has at its center an early Roman funeral relief, re--used here simply as decoration. The relief depicts two men and a woman, probably all of a single family, in the company of the boy god Telesphorus, a chthonic deity (Fig. 5). There is evidence from various parts of the site to show that Telesphorus was worshipped at Stobi along with his father Asclepius and his sister Hygieia from the time of Augustus until at least the middle of the 3rd century.

The small rooms east of the court along the Via Principalis Inferior may have served as storage rooms and one may have an entrance stairway, on the axis of the courtyard, leading up to the street. The complex of rooms on the north includes an entrance onto the Via Axia. The principal rooms of the house are the two apsidal rooms south of the courtyard. The mortar bedding for a mosaic, unfortunately destroyed, was found in the western room, but the eastern room had suffered less and the mosaic pavement there is largely preserved. The floor of the apse was paved with stone slabs so that a rectangular space, ca. 7.5 meters wide and 9.5 meters long, was left for the mosaic.

The rectangular area of the room was divided into nine approximately equal squares with three units in three rows; the entire mosaic was bordered by a cable pattern. Each register in the north and south rows also has an individual border pattern. In the central row the two side panels depict sea creatures in unrestricted space; a man with a trident is also present in the eastern register (Fig. 6). Instead of a central mosaic panel there is a marble encrusted fountain.

A circular medallion containing an inscription is partly preserved in the central register of the northern row at the entrance to the room. Only two words are complete, Περπέτουα and ᾿Ελπιδία (Perpetua and Elpidia); they may be female names. The register to the right contains a stylized kantharos framed by two deer; a tree sprouts from the vessel. The panel to the left has geometric designs and, across the upper part of the panel, is another inscription in Greek.

> ῾Ρουφῖνος Περιστερία
> Περπέτουα Πρώτασις
> ᾿Ελπίδις ᾿Ιωάννης
> Αὐρηλλιανὸς Περιστερία

Rufinus (son of?) Peristerias
Perpetua Protasis
Elpidis Ioannes
Aurellianus (son of?) Peristerias

Lines 2 and 3 of the inscription may be simply a listing of four names but in lines 1 and 4 Peristeria is likely to be the genitive form of Περιστερίας, indicating the name of the father; otherwise we should have to suppose that there were two women named Peristeria referred to in the same inscription. The name is found also in a dedicatory inscription in the earlier mosaic in the south aisle of the Episcopal Basilica (19).

The three southern registers combine tapestry and geometric patterns with small woodland scenes of rampant lions, deer and other animals. These registers are to be especially noted for the quantity of green glass tesserae used to form small motifs.

The mosaic has usually been considered to date to the late 4th or early 5th century and would coincide with the original construction period of the House of Peristerias, at least in its overall form. The house continued in use, with remodelling, at least through the 5th century. The mosaic itself was repaired more than once in antiquity, and different types of materials were employed in patching holes caused by wear or damage.

Rubble walls of earlier Roman constructions have been found below the open courtyard south of the apsidal rooms. Below those structures lies part of the cemetery of the late Hellenistic city. A few graves dating to the 2nd century B.C. were excavated by the Archaeological Museum of Skopje in 1965 and 1966 and four additional graves of the same period were excavated near the south wall of the courtyard in 1972 by the new Stobi Project.

BIBLIOGRAPHY. Dj. Mano-Zissi, "Mosaiken in Stobi", *BIABulg* 10 (1936) 277—297. V. Sokolovska, "Stobi, II: Peristerijeva palata", *Arheološki Pregled* 7 (1965) 128—129. I. Mikulčić, "Stobi — (Peristerija) — kasnohelenistički grobovi", *Arheološki Pregled* 8 (1966) 113—114.

11. VIA THEODOSIA.

This broad (4.5 meters) avenue parallels the Via
Axia and separates the House of Peristerias from the
Theodosian Palace (12). The street was paved with
pebbles and stone slabs and has been covered with
earth to protect the ancient surface. There is an ex-
cellent view of the courtyard and fountain of the
Theodosian Palace from the street.

12. THEODOSIAN PALACE. Fig. 7.

The Emperor Theodosius I visited Stobi in June,
A. D. 388, and issued two edicts regarding the oppres-
sion of heretics and the public discussion of religious topics (Codex Theodosianus 16.4.2, 5.15). While
in Stobi he is likely to have made his quarters in the
largest and most elegant home in the city. The most
likely candidate for that identification among the
houses so far excavated is the lavishly decorated house
lying east of the Via Theodosia. Since the name of
the resident owner is stil unknown to us, the building may be referred to as the Theodosian Palace
in commemoration of the imperial visitor.

The residence is L-shaped, ca. 58 meters long
and 23.5 meters wide (maximum), and is situated
between the Via Principalis Superior and Inferior.
There were at least three entrances to the building.
One (C) opens from the lane that lies south of the

building and leads directly to the south corridor of
the courtyard. An entrance (B) off the Via Principalis
Inferior provides an access to the court that is nearly
as direct: this route passes by the broad entrance to
a square room (1) that may have been a formal reception area, across the width of a long rectangular room
to the corridor that lies behind the east wall of the
courtyard. The third access is the most circu-
itous. A doorway (A) somewhat wider than entrance
(B) leads from the Via Theodosia into a small anteroom from which it is possible, through either of
two doors, to enter the foyer, or reception area just
mentioned.

There may have been a stairway to a second storey to the right of the anteroom of entrance (A). B.
Nestorović, who published the building, restores a
second floor not only above the rooms east of the
courtyard, but to the west as well. He also proposed
an entrance into that level directly from the Via Principalis Superior which lies approximately at the level
of the hypothetical second floor.

The courtyard (2) is lined with colonnades on
the north and west and by a parapet wall on the south.
The columns were re-used here after standing originally in other buildings so that bases of different sizes
were required to equalize the height of the order.
All the column capitals appear to be of a single size
and type. They are of grayish-white marble and fluted spirally in the manner of the pedestals in the
basin and some of the columns. The columns carried

an architrave rather than a series of arches. Along
the east side of the court is a rectangular basin above
which are seven niches framed by green marble co-
lonnettes. Within the basin are eight spirally-fluted
pedestals of grayish-white marble. The statues found
in the basin during the excavations of 1927—1930
must have stood on the pedestals and in the niches.
On each side of the fountain is a small, shallow basin;
each has an apsidal end that projects west beyond
the line of the beginning of the north colonnade.
There are two low platforms on the north and south
sides of the courtyard which may have been used as
garden terraces.

The floor of the courtyard was paved with stone
and marble fragments of different sizes, shapes and
colors, and in the walkways of the peristyle are mosaic pavements of large tesserae arranged in geometric motifs.

A large apsidal room (3), the triclinium, lies at a
slightly higher level to the south. The room is reached by a stairway from the west portico of the courtyard; a rose, brecciated marble threshold for a double door formed the fourth step. The floor of the room
is paved with marble opus sectile bordered by sandstone slabs. The lower parts of the walls were encrusted with marble above which there were frescoes and
wall mosaics. Two rooms, which could be reached
only from the triclinium, lie to the east.

Three of the four rooms west of the portico were
also lavishly decorated. Room 4 (southwest corner)

appears to have been merely an exedra with a bench against three walls. Room 5, which may have been a library, has two semicircular stairways at its entrance, an opus sectile floor, and four columns raised on a platform against the west wall. Room 6 has a mosaic floor with a geometric pattern and the floor of Room 7, which has an apse on the west, is a handsome opus sectile pavement with hexagons and triangles of slate fitted among white marble squares. The facades of all four rooms were encrusted with marble.

A number of statues of the late Hellenistic and Early Imperial periods were found during the excavations. Among the finest of these are two bronze satyrs of the Hellenistic Period (Figs. 8 and 9), two nude marble statues of Aphrodite, and a marble head of Poseidon with gilt hair, all now in the National Museum of Belgrade.

The palace appears to have been constructed in the fourth century. We might suppose it to have been erected towards the middle of the century, before the theater began to be plundered on a large scale for building material, since there is no trace of re-used theater seats anywhere in the building. The geometric patterns of the mosaics in the porticoes of the court-yard, in any case, are not likely to be later than the early 5th century. The palace survived as a residence through much of the 5th century.

BIBLIOGRAPHY. The bibliography for the Theodosian Palace and House of Parthenius is given at the end of the next section.

13. HOUSE OF PARTHENIUS. Fig. 7.

The House of Parthenius is an L-shaped residence on the south side of the Theodosian Palace lying between the triclinium complex of the latter and the Via Principalis Inferior. This smaller residence shares walls with the palace and consequently must be dated to the same early construction period. The palace and the adjacent house were originally published as a single unit, the Palace of Parthenius. There is, however, no direct communication between the two buildings and little reason to suppose that both were occupied by a single family. The name of the residence is derived from the name Παρθενίου on a wheel stamp found in the smaller residence.

The House of Parthenius may be entered from the Via Principalis Inferior (D) or from the lane (E) that lies to the south. Entrance (D) leads via an L--shaped corridor to the northeast corner of a courtyard that is a smaller, less elaborate, version of the courtyard of the Theodosian Palace. There is a water fountain and basin against the west wall, colonnades on the north and east, and a wall on the south. The columns here, however, are crowned with imposts, and once carried an arcade. The imposts, decorated with crosses and rosettes, the columns, and the niches are all carved from the green sandstone that is native to the region of Stobi.

A small apsidal room (8) with an opus sectile floor is on the north side of the courtyard and was entered through double doors with a columnar divider. The column also provided support for the arches of the doorways. A larger rectangular room (9) is entered from the west portico. A mosaic with a series of geometric patterns occupies most of the floor space, and there is a stone-paved platform in the western third of the room which is raised ca. 0.40 meter above the mosaic.

BIBLIOGRAPHY FOR THEODOSIAN PALACE AND HOUSE OF PARTHENIUS. B. N. Nestorović, "Iskopavanja u Stobima", *Starinar* 6 (1931) 109—114; *idem,* "Un palais à Stobi", *Bulgarska akademija na naukite, Sofia* 10 (1936) 173——183. Vl. R. Petković, "Antičke skulpture iz Stobia", *Starinar* 12 (1937) 12—35. Ernst Kitzinger, "A Survey of the Early Christian Town of Stobi", *DOPapers* 3 (1946) 118—129. Dj. Mano-Zissi, "Stobi", *Enciklopedija Jugoslavije* 8, Leksikografski zavod Zagreb (1971) 153—155.

14. VIA PRINCIPALIS SUPERIOR.

The street is only roughly parallel to the Via Principalis Inferior and has been traced from the northwestern corner of the House of Peristerias (10), past the Theodosian Palace (12), to the southwestern corner of the shops alongside the House of the Fuller (15). Beyond the shops, the street assumes a more westerly direction and was lined with colonnades. Although the colonnaded street is an extension of the Via Principalis Superior, its more elaborate nature requires a separate designation. It will be referred to as the Via Sacra.

15. HOUSE OF THE FULLER. Fig. 10.

The House of the Fuller is the name applied to a group of related structures with an architectural history ranging over a period of nearly six centuries. Successive residences and small shops were built above the ruins of the earlier buildings; the builders sometimes utilized parts of the earlier walls, and at other times simply levelled the area. The name given to the area is strictly applicable only to one phase of the small courtyard (4) where a great quantity of murex shells was found that indicated the presence of a cloth dyeing establishment of the 5th century.

The House of the Fuller, which is located west of the Via Principalis Superior near the beginning of the Via Sacra, is still under excavation (1972) and can be presented only summarily here. One of the chief interests for the visitor in viewing the remains is that it is possible to see in this relatively small area parts of buildings from each of the several periods of occupation and to gain some understanding of their spatial and temporal relationships to each other.

a.) The earliest visible remains are parts of rubble walls that may be seen in test trenches within the large apsidal court area (1) and below the floor of Room 2 which lies west of the court. They date to the 1st century after Christ and the structures to which they belonged, probably private residences or small shops, seem to have endured until the early

3rd century. One of the residents of the area made a coin bank from a small jug by cutting a slot in the bottom of the vessel and then planting it, inverted, into a pebble floor. His intentions, however, were evidently stronger than his determination, or greater than his means, for when the vessel was removed during excavations in 1970 the bank was empty.

b.) The area was remodelled greatly in the 3rd century. The apsidal courtyard was constructed, and a stepped entranceway was built for Room 2 which provided access on the left to Room 3 and on the right to another room or court area (unexcavated). Room 3 was heated by the circulation of hot air among brick piers that supported the floor of the room (Fig. 11). The furnace for the room of the hypocaust was in the southwest corner of Room 2. The floor of Room 3 was repaired several times before the hypocaust was abandoned in the early 4th century. During the 4th century a series of four earthen floors were built above each other so that the final floor was nearly 0.40 meter above the first and it was necessary to raise the level of the threshold from Room 2. The final floor was constructed near the end of the century, not long before the destruction of the building by fire.

c.) A rubbish dump of the late 4th and 5th centuries lay above the destruction deposits of the rooms just described, but further west iron workers had a small establishment and an humble residence from the late 4th through much of the 5th century. These structures overlay small residences of the 3rd and 4th centuries which could not be reached directly from the structures already described.

d.) The final period of habitation in the area is just below ground level and dates to the late 5th or early 6th century. Several stone slabs of a floor are visible on the south side of the excavation area; the walls for this building, too, are of roughly worked stones. Sure context for the date of destruction is lacking because of the shallow deposits above the building, but it is likely that the house collapsed during the cataclysm that brought ruin to the city in the last half of the 6th century.

BIBLIOGRAPHY. James Wiseman and Dj. Mano-Zissi, "Excavations at Stobi, 1970", *AJA* 75 (1971) 402—403 and "Excavations at Stobi, 1971", *AJA* 76 (1972) Section 7.

16. EPISCOPAL RESIDENCE.

A series of small rooms extends along the west side of the Via Principalis Superior from the House of the Fuller to its juncture with the Via Sacra (18). On the opposite side of the street are the poorly preserved remains of a building on the approximate level of the street. A broad stairway in the center of the structure leads down to a walkway between two colonnades, the southern of which has a semicircular exedra. The stairs and walkway provide a dramatic approach to a building on the lower terrace.

The colonnaded way leads directly into a rectangular foyer which provides access on the axis into a large apsidal room. There are three smaller rooms on both the north and south sides of the structure. Djordje Mano-Zissi, who excavated the building in 1940, has suggested that it scrvcd as a Christian oratory during the 4th century and was converted into the residence of the bishop in the 5th century. The early date of the original structure is based largely on the style of a number of decorative architectural pieces made of stucco. Among the several objects of an ecclesiastical nature which were found during the excavations are a bronze censer and a golden finger ring with a cross encrusted with four almandines and a pearl in the center.

The Episcopal Residence lies to the north of the great terrace of the Episcopal Basilica. It is likely that a strairway provided access from the residence to the level of the east doorway of the north aisle of the basilica.

Several structures located between the Episcopal Residence and the lane south of the Theodosian Palace (12) and the House of Parthenius (13) were partly excavated in the early 1930s. The most interesting of these is the "prison" area, comprising two vaulted basement rooms where manacled skeletons were discovered in context dating to the 6th century A. C. Above the "prison" a late rubble wall was found which contained a statue base with a lengthy inscription of the 2nd century A. C. recording the priestly services of Claudia Prisca for Artemis Lochia and the Emperors. Most of the wall was removed, but the inscription was left in place. A statuette of Artemis, which may once have stood on the base, was found nearby.

BIBLIOGRAPHY. Dj. Mano-Zissi, "Stukatura u Stobima", *Zbornik Narodnog Muzeja, Beograd* 3 (1962) 101—107. James Wiseman, "Gods, War, and Plague in the Time of the Antonines", in the forthcoming *Studies in the Antiquities of Stobi*, Vol. I, Beograd, 1973.

17. SEMICIRCULAR COURT.

The Via Sacra begins just north of the Semicircular Court which lies opposite the entrance to the Episcopal Basilica. The court is set off from the street by a low parapet made of re-used theater seats with an entrance on its axis. A semicircular colonnade separates the flagstone courtyard from a covered walkway; from the latter there are entrances to 10 or 11 rooms, unexcavated, some of which were certainly shops. Rubble piers were later added in the intercolumniations of the colonnade.

A base for a large monument is partly preserved in the center of the courtyard and it has been suggested that it once carried an equestrian statue of the father of the Emperor Theodosius I, the latter of whom visited Stobi in A. D. 388.

The construction of the court may be contemporary with the Episcopal Basilica in the late 4th or

towns and the basilica appears to have been imposed on that plan. The difference in orientation may have been the result of a desire to lay out the axis of the church at sunrise on the day of whatever saint was the patron of the church. According to calculations in an unpublished paper by Mr. Živojin Radošević, the orientation indicates that the church was laid out on October 26, St. Demetrius' Day. But it is also possible that the basilica assumed the orientation of an earlier holy spot (pagan or Christian) or that the terrace was simply forced into available space. In any case, an irregularly shaped atrium was necessary to provide a transition from the Via Sacra to the narthex of the church.

The narthex has a door on the north leading to a complex of two rooms and a stairway to the second floor. A door in the south wall leads to a broad, sandstone stairway that descends to the level of the Baptistery. There is a door for each of the two side aisles and a broad central entrance to the nave. The lintel of the nave was carved with an inscription commemorating the construction of the church by Bishop Philip.

᾿Εμμανουήλ + μεθ' ἡμῶν ὁ θ(εό)ς
ὁ ἁγιώτατος ἐπίσκοππος Φίλιππος + οἰκοδομὴ ἐν τὴν ἁγίαν
τοῦ θ(εο)ῦ ἐκκλησίαν

"Emmanuel. God (is) with us.
The most holy Bishop Philip (brought about) a building for the holy church of God."

The lintel was broken into two parts at the time of the destruction of the building, and the fragments recovered at different times. Half of the lintel is now in the National Museum of Belgrade and the other half has been placed in the south aisle of the basilica.

The main body of the basilica consists of a wide, central nave separated from the two side aisles by colonnades. The columns are crowned by acanthus capitals, often with peacocks and other birds sculpted among the leaves. Imposts rested on the capitals and carried an arcade above which stood the unfluted Ionic columns and screens of the second storey. There is a single apse with a sunken confessio and ambulatory behind the presbyterium.

Two phases of the presbyterium are visible. The earlier is represented by a base for a chancel scereen, made of re-used theater seats, that extended entirely across the width of the nave. The pink mortar bedding of this early phase, almost certainly contemporary with the earlier mosaic in the south aisle, preserves the impressions of the opus sectile floor with which it was originally paved. The later presbyterium had a slate floor at a slightly higher level and the chancel screen returned on both sides to leave narrow passages between the colonnades and the screen. The base just mentioned was built largely of rose colored, brecciated marble, but theater seats were also used on the sides. The seats for the clergy that framed the east side of the presbyterium may have been in use during both phases.

The floor of the nave was paved during one of its periods with marble and slate opus sectile but was later covered with sandstone slabs. The ambo (pulpit) was an elaborately carved construction of marble with two stairways that stood on a base of roseate, brecciated marble, at least some of which had been taken from an earlier inscribed monument. Most of the final chancel screen, the marble sides of the ambo, and many of the capitals from the colonnades are now in the National Museum at Belgrade.

Parts of three superimposed floor pavements were found in the south aisle of the basilica. The earliest is a mosaic with geometric patterns that extended from the south wall to the south colonnade. A dedicatory legend was uncovered in this mosaic in 1970 and a second inscription in 1972. The first states simply, in Greek characters, "Peristerias (or Peristeria: the final letters are lost) made it (i. e., the mosaic) because of a vow." The more recently discovered inscription lies near the eastern end of the aisle.

ὑπὲρ εὐ[χῆς]
τῆς ματ[ρώνας]
ἡ εὐλαβ[εστά-]
τη διακ[όνισσα]
τὴν ἐξέ[δραν]
ἐψήφω[σεν]

"Because of a vow
of the Matron,

the most pious
deaconess
paved the exedra
with mosaic."

The exedra, presumably, is the area at the eastern end of the south aisle.

Both the mosaic just described and the floor of the earlier presbyterium were badly disturbed and their surfaces wrinkled, probably by an earthquake. When the new presbyterium was constructed a second mosaic was laid in the south aisle, which extended from the basilica wall to a new base for a mullioned screen set a short distance south of the colonnade. The north aisle must have undergone a similar remodelling. A part of the later mosaic was discovered near the east end of the south aisle in 1972, but was very badly preserved and has been removed for reconstitution in the Museum. The design is a lively, colorful one of animals in combat in one register while a second panel depicts sea creatures (Fig. 12). During a third and final phase the floor of the aisle was covered with sandstone slabs, a few o which were found in place above the later mosaic.

The animal figures of the second mosaic in the south aisle have stylistic features similar to figures in the mosaic of the narthex, which was uncovered during excavations in the early part of this century. But there are geometric motifs in the narthex also that are nearly identical with the earlier mosaic. It is possible that the two mosaics were created at times not greatly distant from each other. The second mosaic belongs to the 5th century, while the first mosaic was laid in the late 4th or early 5th century. Several coins were found in the mortar *between* the levels of the two mosaics, including one dating to the reign either of Honorius or of Theodosius III (A. D. 408—423). The floor of sandstone slabs probably belongs to the 6th century and was in use when the basilica collapsed sometime not long after A. D. 569/70, the date of the latest coin found below destruction debris on the south side of the basilica.

The walls of the narthex and the aisles of the basilica were covered at least in part with fresco, some of which included figures of saints and animals. Most of these pieces were recovered during the early excavations and are in the National Museum at Belgrade, but a few more figured fragments were recovered in the excavations of 1970 in the destruction debris of the south wall of the basilica. Fragments of wall mosaics, including gilded glass tesserae, have also been found.

BIBLIOGRAPHY. R. Egger, "Gradska crkva u Stobima", *Glasnik Skopskog naučnog društva* 5 (1929) 14—44; *idem.*, "Die städtische Kirche von Stobi", *JÖAI* 24 (1929) 42—87. B. Saria, "Novi nalasci u episkopskoj crkvi u Stobima", *Glasnik Skopskog naučnog društva* 12 (1933) 1—22; *idem,* "Neue Funde in der Bischofskirche von Stobi", *JÖAI* 28 (1933) 112—139. Ernst Kitzinger, "A Survey of the Early Christian Town of Stobi", *DOPapers* 3 (1946) 87—110. R. F. Hoddinott, *Early Byzantine*

Churches in Macedonia and Southern Serbia (London and New York 1963) 161—167. James Wiseman and Dj. Mano-Zissi "Excavations at Stobi, 1970", *AJA* 75 (1971) 398—401 and "Excavations at Stobi, 1971" *AJA* 76 (1972) Section 8.

20. BAPTISTERY.

The stairway that descends from the south door of the narthex of the Episcopal Basilica leads to a series of chambers whose functions are as yet unclear. They may have served as antechambers for the Baptistery which occupies, approximately, the mid-part of the space along the south side of the basilica. The Baptistery was discovered only in 1971 and the adjoining rooms have not yet all been excavated, so that it is not yet possible to say whether the chief access to the Baptistery lay to the east or west.

The plan of the Baptistery is essentially a quatrefoil with small corner apses inscribed within a quadrangle that is almost square, ca. 9.4 meters to a side. Its north wall is built flush against the south terrace wall of the basilica. There is an entrance at each corner of the Baptistery, at least two of which (NE and NW) were spanned by brick and concrete arches, and there is a broader doorway on the south.

A large circular piscina (interior diameter 2.4 meters) is centered in the room. The piscina had a brick parapet that rose over 60 centimeters above the floor and was faced with slate and vari-colored marble slabs. Four stairways originally descended from the top of the parapet to the floor of the piscina, a depth of 1.33 meters. The southwestern stairway, however, was removed and a large marble kantharos (0.94 meter high) was set into its place in the later 5th or early 6th century. The parapet also carried six small, unfluted, but brightly painted columns which supported a baldacchino.

Water was supplied to the piscina from the south by a lead pipe laid in a narrow channel. The water evidently arrived with sufficient force to rise through a hollow marble cylinder, spirally fluted on the exterior, in the center of the floor of the piscina. How the piscina was drained is not yet clear.

The floor of the Baptistery was paved with a mosaic (Fig. 13). There is a band of running spirals along the walls, around the piscina, and between the four main panels. Each of the panels dips towards one of the corners and depicts water fowl gathered about deer and peacocks who are drinking from an overflowing kantharos. There are geometric patterns in each of the doorways and in two semi-circular niches of the piscina. The technical quality of the mosaic is high and the design concept is pleasing. There can be little doubt that its creator was the same artist(s) who designed the mosaic in the triclinium of the House of Psalms (5).

Six unfluted columns with composite capitals stood on Ionic bases on the mosaic floor close against the wall of the parapet during the last phase of the

Baptistery. They would have helped support the central roof structure.

Thousands of fragments of the fresco that once covered the walls of the Baptistery were recovered during the excavations of 1971. The material is still being cleaned, examined and mended, but as of 1972, 20 expressive portrait faces in a variety of poses and sizes have been recovered. The sensitive features of the youth in Fig. 14 are evidence of the skill and creativity of the painter. Several of the faces are characterized by the sideways-glance already encountered among the faces from the fresco of the narthex of the Episcopal Basilica. The similarities, indeed, are striking and suggest not only contemporaneity, but even the same painter, or at least the same school. Other fresco fragments include parts of bodies and drapery.

The figured fresco had been covered over by a later coating of stucco before the final destruction of the Baptistery. Only a few pieces of painted stucco were found on the wall at the time of excavation, and these all displayed simple geometric motifs.

The small room to the south of the Baptistery, where several periods of use are also evident in wall patches and superimposed floor levels, contained what may have been a collecting tank and drain for holy water, or some other liquid. The drain begins near the northwest corner of the room beneath the point in the Baptistery wall where a small lead pipe was discovered. In addition, over 100 coins, ranging in date from the mid-4th to the mid-5th centuries after Christ, were found in the soft earth fill above the small basin and drain. Such a large number of coins from such a small area is highly unlikely to be the result of accidental loss, nor is there any indication that the coins belong to a single hoard. The conclusion seems inescapable that the coins were deliberately placed, probably tossed, in the vicinity of the drain over a period of some years during the life of the Baptistery. The entire area was covered over by an earthen floor by the end of the 5th century. Coins and other material found above the final floor date to the 6th century.

The partially-blocked entrance to a large, vaulted crypt, which was built into the terrace wall for the basilica, lies just outside the northwest doorway of the Baptistery. The crypt, plundered in antiquity, was probably the tomb of one of the bishops of Stobi (perhaps the builder, Philip), or of a martyr.

There is a large room to the east of the Baptistery which is still (1972) under excavation. An arch springs from the south wall of the basilica to a pier that is located on the axis of the Baptistery. Another arch presumably spanned the distance to the south. A low bench runs along the outside of the Baptistery wall and there is a plastered earth socle for a decorative member at its southern end beside the doorway. The excavators plan eventually to uncover not only the rest of this room, but all the structures that lie along the south side of the basilica.

The Baptistery with its mosaic, and probably the figured wall fresco, date to the late 4th or early 5th century after Christ. The patches in the mosaic floor, in the piscina and in the walls of the adjacent room, as well as the covering of the original fresco, all testify to a series of remodelling that extended into the 6th century. The Baptistery was abandoned for at least a short time before its final destruction: the crypt was robbed and the mosaic was hacked through for the sole purpose of removing the lead water pipe, of which a few small scraps were found during excavations.

There was no disturbance of the ruins after the Baptistery and the basilica collapsed either in an earthquake, or when they were deliberately destroyed by fire set by invaders. The latest coins found on the floors of the Baptistery and adjacent rooms, beneath the destruction debris, date to the third quarter of the 6th century.

BIBLIOGRAPHY. James Wiseman and Dj. Mano-Zissi, "Excavations at Stobi, 1971", *AJA* 76 (1972) Section 9.

21. PORTA HERACLEA.

The only gate of the city that has been discovered so far lies at the southwestern end of the Via Sacra. The road to Heraclea Lyncestis probably began at this point. The central area of the gateway and the upper part of the city wall were cleared during the 1930s, and in 1972 excavation was resumed on a small scale west of the inner gate.

The Porta Heraclea may properly be called a dipylon, that is, a double gateway. The distance between the thresholds of the two gates is nearly 9 meters and the width of the inner threshold is 3.25 meters. Walls perpendicular to the line of the City Wall close the space of the dipylon on the east and west and there were at least two rectangular rooms on each side of the central passage. The rooms must have been roofed, but the passage seems to have been open to the sky. The early excavators found evidence for an arch, crowned by a marble cornice, over the gate on the city side; a similar structure is likely over the outer gate.

Remains of a second wall, perhaps a *proteichisma*, can be seen abutting the outer gate on the east and west and lying parallel to the City Wall. Several theater seats were built into the wall, but this feature is little help in dating since architectural members from the theater were being re-used from at least the late 4th century.

We cannot yet date the several phases of construction of the Porta Heraclea, but it is now possible to say something about its destruction. During the 1972 excavations, debris from the collapse of the city wall where it joins the Porta on the west was removed from a small room built against the City Wall and entered from the colonnade beside the inner gate.

The latest coin found in the destruction debris near the floor of the room dates to the 6th century A. C.

BIBLIOGRAPHY. Dj. Mano-Zissi, "Iskopavanja u Stobima 1933 i 1934 godine", *Starinar* 10—11 (1935—36) 145—50; *idem*, "Bemerkungen über die altbyzantinische Stadt von Stobi", *Atti del Ve Congresso Internazionale di Studi Bizantine* 2 (1940) 225—227. Ernst Kitzinger, "A Survey of the Early Christian Town of Stobi", *DOPapers* 3 (1946) 110—114.

22. WEST CEMETERY.

A large, rectangular trench, 9 meters wide by nearly 12 meters long, was dug in 1970—1971, not far to the southwest of the Porta Heraclea, to investigate a part of what has been designated the West Cemetery. A total of 81 graves were excavated here in two seasons.

The earliest graves belong to the late 1st century B. C. / early 1st century A. C., and they lay either on, or partly within virgin soil. The cemetery continued in use, with an interruption in the late 2nd and early 3rd centuries, until the 4th century. The latest graves were all inhumation burials in shallow pits while the earlier burials included both cremation and inhumation.

Funeral offerings were more numerous in the early graves and included coins, ceramic vessels, iron strigils, terracotta and glass unguentaria, jewelery, and terracotta figurines. A cremation burial of Augustan date (Grave 21) excavated in 1970 contained, among other gifts, several figurines of the boy-god Telesphorus (Fig. 15) and in 1971 another cremation burial of the same date (Grave 76) was discovered which contained nearly 60 figurines of a variety of types.

The West Cemetery may be said to extend to the southwest at least as far as the Cemetery Basilica (28) where a small test in 1972 revealed several graves of the early 1st century A. C. Other burials of both early and late Roman times have been found occasionally still further to the southwest, some of them more than a kilometer from the Porta Heraclea.

The Stobi Museum contains a special display of a cremation burial of the late 1st century A. C. as well as displays showing forms of burials in the West Cemetery. Many of the figurines and other objects found in the cemetery are also on exhibit in the Museum.

BIBLIOGRAPHY. James Wiseman and Djordje Mano--Zissi, "Excavations at Stobi, 1970", *AJA* 75 (1971) 403—406 and "Excavations at Stobi, 1971", *AJA* 76 (1972) Section 5. Ivan Mikulčić, "The West Cemetery: Excavations in 1965" and Al B. Wesolowsky, "Burial Customs in the West Cemetery", in the forthcoming *Studies in the Antiquities of Stobi*, Vol. 1.

23. THEATER.

The theater (Fig. 16) was built in the 2nd or early 3rd century A. C. to a design that closely resembles earlier Greek structures. The principal units of the theater, cavea, orchestra and scene building, are separate in form; and the scene building has no stage, but an elaborate facade as a background to the performances that took place in the orchestra.

The cavea, which originally had two tiers, was built of grayish-white marble brought from quarries in the region of the Pletvar Pass to the southwest of Stobi. The lower tier, nearly half of which is still preserved, has eight stairways and 17 rows of seats (Fig. 17). A diazoma, or central walkway, separated the two tiers and would have been located directly above the outer wall of the central annular corridor. Windows were cut through the vertical faces of several seats in the 16th row to provide light and ventilation for the interior corridor. The upper tier would have had 19 rows of seats and 15 stairways. We may assume that a second horizontal passage existed at the top of the theater at the back of the upper tier.

William B. Dinsmoor, Jr., who drew the plan published in Fig. 16, has recently estimated a total seating capacity of 7,638. Many of the patrons of the theater, especially during the 3rd century, recorded their names on the seats. Citizens seem to have advertised their right to sit in a particular spot by carving either their initials or some fuller form of their name, almost always in the genitive, on the vertical face, or on the lip, or the horizontal surface of the seat. Both Roman and Greek names are written in Greek characters.

Seats were evidently alloted by tribal member-
ship for the names of five tribes are also inscribed in
the cavea: Terentia, Valeria, Martia, Mercuria, and
Vibia. The name of each tribe (phyle) that is preserved was written on the lip of a seat. The tribal name
Vibia, with a different spelling, may be repeated on
a horizontal surface. Terentia is also recorded in red
paint on the vertical balustrade of the theater.

The orchestra is larger than a semicircle and is
somewhat irregular in contour. There is as yet no
evidence that the orchestra was ever paved. There
are parodoi on both sides of the orchestra separating
the cavea from the scene building; they sloped gen-
tly towards the orchestra. The analemma, or supporting wall for the cavea, in both parodoi is preserved
nearly to the top of the first tier of seats. It is likely
that much of the cavea was free-standing, so that a
supporting wall would have been needed for its entire
perimeter.

The scene building was a large structure extending well beyond the limits of the orchestra to provide
at its extremities a facing wall for the parodoi. A two-
-storied *scaenae frons* masked the central structure.
There were five doorways in the lower storey of
the *scaenae frons*, each one reached by a flight of stairs.
Between the stairways pedestals carried marble Corinthian columns in pairs in front of Corinthian pilas-
ters; there were additional columns on the ends.
The epistyle-frieze course was continuous above the
columns and doorways, and carried a second smaller

order of Corinthian columns on single pedestals. The columns of the *scaenae frons* are of rose and green brecciated marble, while the fine-grained white marble of the capitals, the epistyle, and other architectural pieces may be Pentelic from Attica in Greece.

The theater was converted into an arena for wild animal and gladiatorial combat, probably in the later 3rd century, by the addition of a rubble wall in front of the *scaenae frons* to provide a *via venatorum* at orchestra level in front of the scene building, and by adding a parapet of similar construction on top of the balustrade at the level of the first row of seats. The parodoi, too, were closed by gates, perhaps of wood. Inside the scene building the central room was converted into a sanctuary of Nemesis. Part of a female votive statue and part of the face of the statue of Nemesis, as well as dedicatory inscriptions, were recovered by the excavators in the 1920s and 1930s.

Perhaps the most interesting piece of sculpture found in the theater, however, is a nearly complete torso of an emperor wearing a cuirass that was found during work in the theater in 1967. The statue (Fig. 18) is now on exhibit in the Stobi Museum.

The theater-arena probably went out of use shortly after the Emperor Constantine issued an imperial decree forbidding gladiatorial and wild animal fights (A. D. 325, Codex Theodosianus 15.12.1). The parodoi began to be filled with rubbish heaps before the middle of the century, which by the end of the century had reached a depth of over three meters. A number of small houses with wall socles of rubble were built above the rubbish dump, along the slopes to the east and even against the back wall of the scene building.

A large part of the *scaenae frons* had collapsed into the orchestra before the deep fill began to accumulate there, but it is not known whether the collapse was brought about by deliberate destruction or by earthquake. In any case, many of the architectural pieces were evidently covered over before the theater began to be used as a ready supply of worked stone. The entire upper tier and much of the lower tier of the cavea were eventually quarried away to provide building material for structures erected in the late 4th century, throughout the 5th century, and into the last century of occupation. Theater seats or other architectural members from the theater are visible now in the Outer City Wall near the Porta Heraclea, in shops and pedestals along the Via Sacra, the Semicircular Court, the Episcopal Basilica, near the Casino, in the Central Fountain, in the Synagogue Basilica, the North Basilica and even in the new stretch of the Inner City Wall excavated in 1972 (25).

BIBLIOGRAPHY. B. Saria, *Pozorište u Stobima* in *Godišnjak muzeja Južne Srbije* I (1937) 1—68; *idem*, "Das Theater von Stobi", *AA* (1938) 81—148; *idem.*, "Die Inschriften des Theaters von Stobi", *WJh* 32 (1940) 1—34. E. Dyggve, "Le théâtre mixte du bas-empire d'apres le théâtre de Stobi et les diptyques consulaires", *RA* (1958) pt. 1, pp. 137—157, pt. 2, pp. 20—39. F. Papazoglu, "Natpis iz Nemezejona i datovanje Stobskog Pozorišta", *Živa Antika* 1 (1951) 279—293. James Wiseman and Djordje Mano-Zissi, "Excavations at Stobi, 1970", *AJA* 75 (1971) 402 and "Excavations at Stobi, 1971", *AJA* 76 (1972) Section 6.

24. CASINO. Fig. 19.

Just prior to the outbreak of World War II part of a building that lies immediately beyond the entrance to the north parodos of the theater was explored under the direction of Dj. Mano-Zissi. Its chief entrance was probably from the Via Principalis Inferior (9), but only the central part of the building toward the east was excavated.

The principal room so far uncovered is a large, rectangular room with an apse on the east. There is a bench against the wall of the apse and a marble table set into the floor on the axis of the room, also in the apse. The marble may have served as a gaming table; several dice and a bronze tray, perhaps for tossing the dice, were found together on the floor near-by. There is also a small fountain in the center of the room. A room northeast of the apsidal room has a door on the east which may lead to the exterior.

There is a corridor to the west where part of a mosaic pavement with geometric designs is preserved. Other rooms further west and to the south have not been excavated. North of the apsidal room is a chamber with a marble floor pavement and marble

revetment on the walls. There is a total of four bathing
cubicles, large enough only for one or two persons
each, set into the west, north, and east walls. A colonnaded sitting room, also with a marble floor and walls,
is raised one step above the level of the bathing room
on the south. This elegant suite suggests that enter-
tainment other than gambling may have been available to the patrons.

The building was in existence during the Late
Roman period, but further excavation will be required to determine its date of construction.

25. INNER CITY WALL.

The line of the Inner City Wall can be followed
on the ground along a low ridge stretching from near
the southeast corner of the Museum to the Outer
City Wall southwest of the theater (See Plan of Site).
The wall has been revealed in only one area: a section
(25) to the east of the Synagogue Basilica (4) was
excavated in 1972. That excavation, coupled with
evidence from excavations in 1970 and 1971 in the
vicinity of the East City Wall near the Crna River
(26), has suggested that the Inner City Wall may,
in fact, be simply the later City Wall in that area.
The part of the city nearest the Crna appears to have
been abandoned in the 4th century A. C. either because of heavy destruction during an invasion, or
because of repeated flooding of the area by the river,

or both. Further excavation is required to clarify the chronology and the circumstances of construction.

The wall is 2.36 meters thick in its upper part and preserved to a height of nearly 3 meters above the probable ground level at the time of construction. The trench for the heavy substructure of the wall was cut through the destruction deposit of a building with a mosaic floor which lies 4.75 meters below the highest preserved part of the wall on the east. The wall foundation extends even below the mosaic.

The ruins of a building with a narrow stairway descending to a brick and concrete archway at a level more than 1.5 meters below that of the mosaic floor were found west of the Inner Wall in 1972. The stairway had originally been covered by a concrete vault rising from massive walls, the latter of which are preserved. The structure may be related to the room with the mosaic found east of the Inner Wall.

26. EAST CITY WALL AND TURKISH BRIDGE.

The outer wall of the city can be followed almost entirely around the perimeter of the site. It encloses an area ca. 400 meters east-west by nearly 450 meters north-south (see Plan of Site). Sections of the outer wall have been uncovered, or have always been visible, high on the ridge overlooking the Vardar River; at the Porta Heraclea (21); southeast of the Porta Heraclea near the excavation storage houses where the interior of a tower over 4 meters deep was excavated in the 1930s; and at several points along the Crna River.

A stone-paved ramp dating to the period of the Turkish domination of Macedonia was cleared in 1971 on the left bank of the Crna. (The ramp and the area of the structures described here are indicated by the numeral 26 on the Site Plan.) The ramp now ends above an abutment made of large stone blocks, but during its period of use provided access to a bridge across the Crna. Two ruined stone piers, prow--shaped on the sides that face the current, and the bridge abutment on the right bank are still visible. (Ruins of a bridge spanning the Vardar were noted by early excavators at Stobi. There are extensive remains of a town on the left bank of the Vardar to which the bridge presumably provided access, but the date neither of bridge nor of town is known.)

The Turkish ramp was built across the line of the City Wall but at a higher level, and in 1970 a section of the City Wall was excavated immediately to the north of the ramp. The wall was constructed of roughly-shaped stones and re-used blocks set in mortar. The thickness of the wall here is 2.3 meters and it is preserved to a height of 3.75 meters on the exterior. A test trench against the inner face revealed a floor of large stone slabs built against the wall. Pottery found immediately above the floor dated chiefly to the 3rd century A. C.

Part of a large building, with walls preserved to a height of over three meters, was excavated a short distance to the north of the ramp in 1970—1972. Several rooms have now been located but the floor lies below the water table of the area and has been reached (1972) in only one small test trench. The walls of three of the rooms are faced with molded stucco panels that may have been in the process of being resurfaced at the time the building was abandoned in the later 4th century.

The City Wall here went out of use by sometime in the late 4th or 5th century A. C. when a rubble wall less than a meter wide and bedded partly on earth was constructed above it.

BIBLIOGRAPHY. James Wiseman and Djordje Mano--Zissi, "Excavations at Stobi, 1971", *AJA* 76 (1972) Section 4.

27. MUSEUM.

The Stobi Museum was opened on August 5, 1972, by the City of Titov Veles and the Stobi Excavation Project. The Museum is currently housed in one room of the former railway station: the rest of the building is used as a storage area for contextual material and during excavation seasons serves as the study area for field archaeologists.

The initial exhibit in the Museum was arranged by both American and Yugoslavian members of the 1972 excavation staff. The material is arranged in displays intended to show various aspects of life in

the ancient city from Hellenistic times to the Early
Christian period; the chronological arrangement of the
displays in the room is counterclockwise. Photographs
and maps are included in the exhibits both to locate
the different parts of the site and to give some indication of the circumstances in which the artifacts
displayed were actually discovered.

The following is a brief description of the nature
of the main exhibits.

North Wall. A general photograph of the site and
maps of the area and site are displayed on the wall.

West Wall. Case 1 contains artifacts dating from
the 3rd century B. C. to the early 1st century A. C.,
including ceramic vessels, glass perfume bottles, coins,
lamps, household implements, and jewelery. The case
also contains a part of the great Roman denarii hoard
found in 1971 below the synagogue (4). A statuette
of Asclepius stands on a console at the center of the
wall above an inscription recording a dedication to
Asclepius, Hygieia and Telesphorus. Case 2 in the
wall niche contains terracotta figurines found in
graves dating to the time of Augustus. Among the many
types of terracottas are figures of Telesphorus, Aphrodite, Europa on a bull, and a faun playing a lyre.

South Wall. Case 3 contains a reconstitution of
Grave 39, a cremation burial of the late 1st century
A. C. Photographs above the case illustrate the different forms of graves found at Stobi. The marble
statue of a draped woman dating to the early years

of the Roman Empire was found by farmers at the near-by village of Rosoman.

East Wall. The 3rd century synagogue of Polycharmus and its 4th century successor are represented by decorative stucco moldings, fresco, and transcriptions of the Polycharmus Inscription. The 5th century mosaic from the adjacent House of Psalms is shown in a large photograph. Case 4 contains artifacts dating chiefly from the late 1st to mid-4th centuries A. C. Of special interest are the coins minted at Stobi, the numerous moldmade terracotta lamps with relief disks, and the several tools and implements of bone, bronze, and iron. Case 5 contains artifacts from the latest phase of urban life at Stobi, late 4th to 6th centuries A. C. One of the portrait heads from the Baptistery fresco is exhibited and above the case are photographs of the Baptistery.

Center. Sections of mosaics from the 4th century synagogue and from the Episcopal Basilica are in the center of the room. The statue of a Roman emperor was found in the theater in 1967.

OUTLYING AREAS

28. CEMETERY BASILICA. Fig. 20.

The Cemetery Basilica is located ca. 250 meters southwest of the Porta Heraclea near the modern cart road to the v llage of Palikura. The building has a narthex, apsidal nave, and two side aisles. The nave is unusual in having two semicircular, concentric apses. There is an additional pair of rooms on both the north and south sides of the nave. The entrance to the basilica was not determined by the excavators, but may have been through a rectangular room on the north side from which a broad doorway opens into one of the rooms north of the narthex.

Numerous graves were found below the floor of the church and some of them evidently ante-date the construction of the basilica. A few other graves, including vaulted tombs, were excavated outside the limits of the building. A mosaic revealed by the excavators of the basilica in 1918 was destroyed not long after its discovery. The published photograph of the mosaic shows that it was nearly identical with the earlier mosaic excavated in 1970 and 1972 in the south aisle of the Episcopal Basilica, and so should also date to the late 4th or early 5th century A. C.

A well-preserved underground crypt, probably a martyrium, was excavated in 1937 south of the narthex.

BIBLIOGRAPHY. H. Dragendorff, "Archäologische und kunstwissenschaftliche Arbeit während des Weltkrieges in Mazedonien", *Zeitschrift für Bildende Kunst* 54 (1919) 259—270. Ć. Truhelka, "Arheološke beleške iz južne Srbije", *Glasnik Skopskog naučnog društva* 3 (1937) 78—81. R. F. Hoddinott, *Early Byzantine Churches in Macedonia and Southern Serbia* (London and New York 1963) 167—168. James Wiseman and Djordje Mano-Zissi, "Excavations at Stobi, 1970", *AJA* 75 (1971) 403—404.

29. PALIKURA BASILICA. Fig. 21.

A basilica is located ca. 2 kilometers south of the Porta Heraclea near the bridge that carries the cart road across the Crna River to the village of Palikura. The basilica was excavated in 1916. The building has a narthex with entrances to the side aisles and the central apsidal nave. The nave is separated from the aisles by colonnades of five columns on each side.

The apse projects eastward into a small courtyard, in the northeast corner of which is an octagonal baptistery set within a square building. There are other annexes to the church which suggest that the basilica belonged to a monastic complex. The basilica may have been constructed in the 5th century and was remodelled extensively in the mid-6th century.

The presence of the baptistery is curious because two others exist within the city and baptism in the early church was normally performed only by the bishop. The question of whether or not all the baptisteries were contemporary has been raised, but unfortunately the dating both of the Palikura Basilica and the North Basilica (1) has been based chiefly on the style of the sculptured architecture. The available archaeological evidence suggests that the use periods of all three baptisteries at least overlap. It is possible that one or both of the baptisteries in the two smaller basilicas belonged to a sect apart from the orthodox church represented by the Episcopal Basilica with its grand baptistery (19—20). It is also possible that the demands for baptism were simply too great to be met by a single bishop and his baptistery, so that permission to perfrom the rite may have been extended to other clergy in the city.

BIBLIOGRAPHY. Dr. Hald, *Auf den Trümmern Stobis* (Stuttgart 1917) 29—41. R. F. Hoddinott, *Early Christian Churches in Macedonia and Southern Serbia* (London and New York 1963) 185—186.

FIGURES

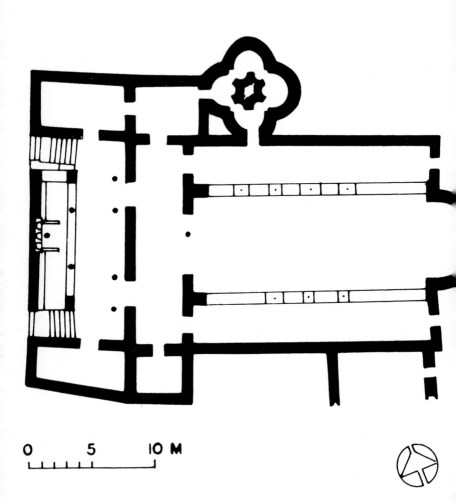

0   5   10 M

Fig. 1

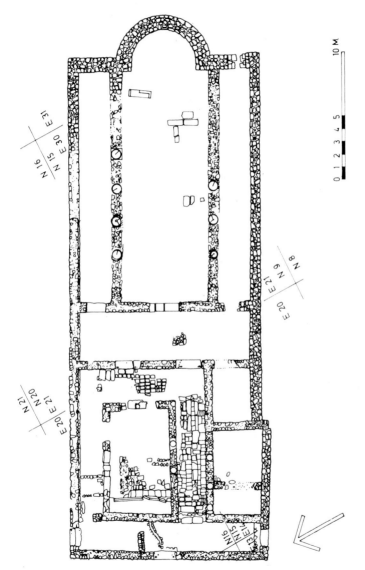

Fig. 2

Fig. 3

Fig. 4

Fig. 5

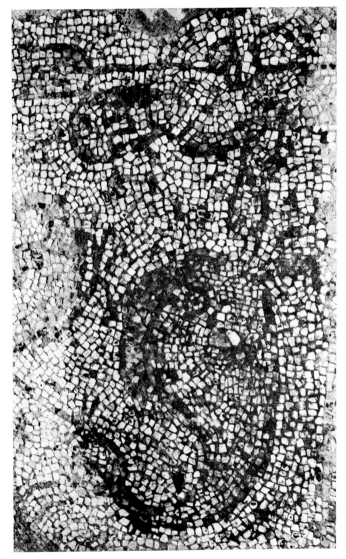

Fig. 6

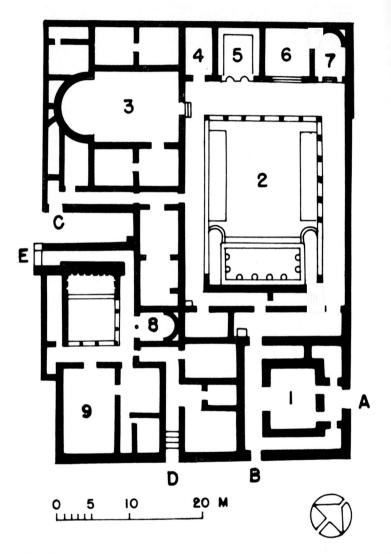

Fig. 7

Fig. 8

Fig. 9

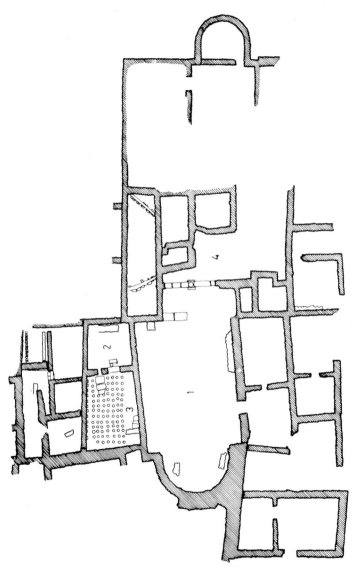

Fig. 10

Fig. 11

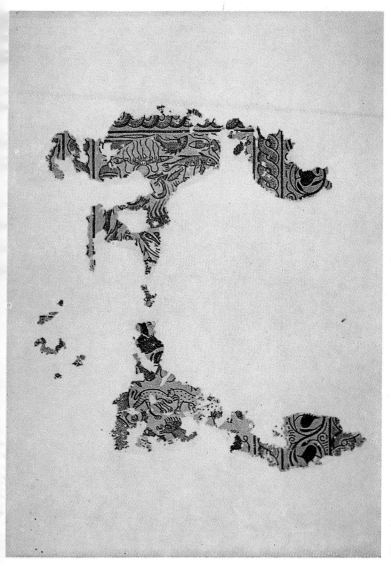

Fig. 12

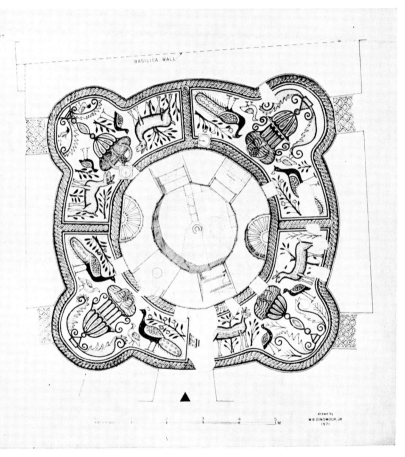

BASILICA WALL

drawn by
W B DINSMOOR, JR
1971

Fig. 13

Fig. 14

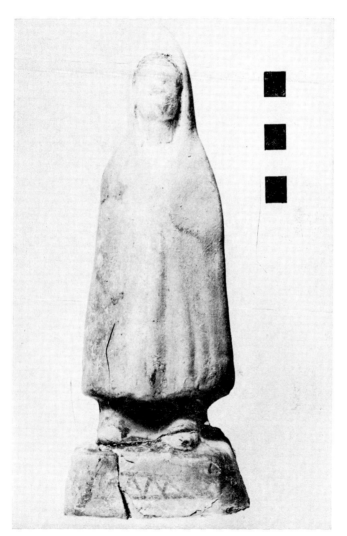

Fig. 15

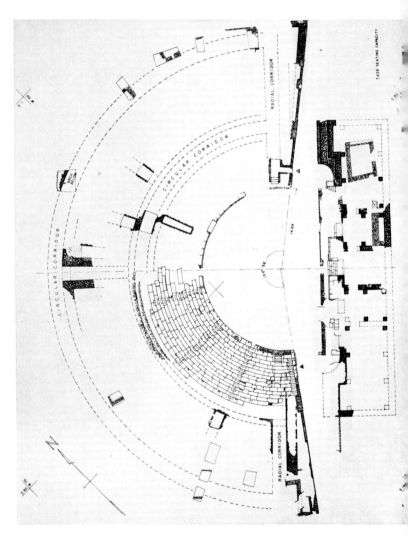

Fig. 16

Fig. 17

Fig. 18

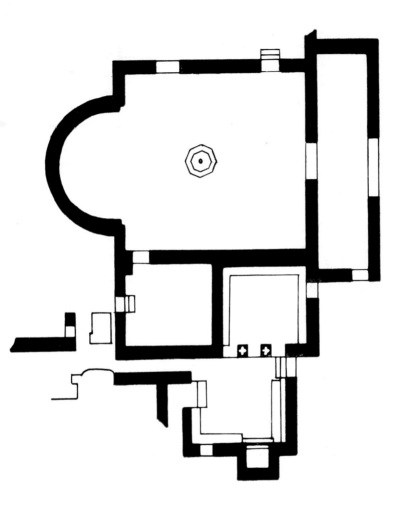

0   5   10 M

Fig. 19

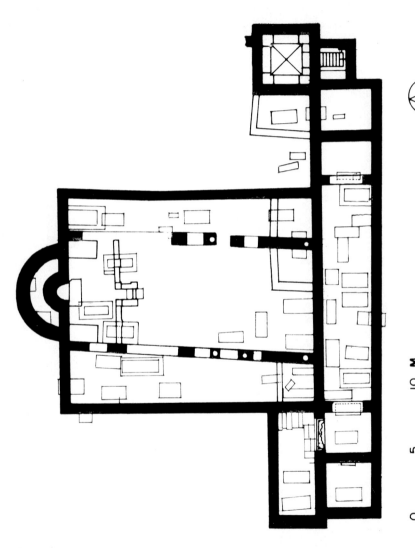

Fig. 20